Marshmallows

Contents

Mad about
MARSHMALLOWS

Introduction

MARSHMALLOWS ARE THE HOTTEST NEW TREND IN THE WORLD OF HOMEMADE CONFECTIONERY—IF YOU THOUGHT THESE LIGHT-AS-AIR PILLOWS OF SUGARY SWEETNESS WERE TOO DIFFICULT TO MAKE YOURSELF, THEN THINK AGAIN!

All of the marshmallows in this book are based on one basic recipe. Hone your mallow-making skills and familiarize yourself with the terminology and techniques using the basic recipe (page 12), then expand your repertoire to include the more indulgent variations that follow. With a huge selection of shapes, flavors, and finishing flourishes (which you can pick and mix to create your own maverick marshmallows) you really are spoiled for choice.

Top tips for sweet success

MARSHMALLOW MAKING IS ALL DOWN TO TIMING SO IT'S ESSENTIAL TO HAVE EVERYTHING READY BEFORE YOU START. FIRST PREPARE THE PAN OR MOLDS, THEN ACCURATELY MEASURE ALL THE INGREDIENTS. DISSOLVE THE GELATIN WHILE THE SUGAR SYRUP IS BOILING, THEN JUST BEFORE THE SYRUP REACHES THE FIRM BALL STAGE, START BEATING THE EGG WHITES.

◯ **To achieve a crystal-clear syrup, make sure that the sugar is completely dissolved in the liquid before slowly bringing it to a boil. Don't stir a boiling syrup, because this will make it become cloudy and grainy.**

◯ **When dissolving the gelatin, use hot (not boiling) liquid and stir for 1-2 minutes, until the grains have dissolved. If any small lumps of gelatin remain, place the bowl into a larger bowl of hot water and stir until the liquid is clear.**

◯ **Add the hot syrup and gelatin to the beaten egg whites in a slow and steady stream. Try to make sure the syrup hits the egg whites and not the beater attachments or the sides of the bowl where it will set instantly.**

◯ **When all the syrup has been beaten into the egg whites, increase the speed of the mixer and beat continuously for about 10 minutes—the mixture will increase in volume and become thick and glossy.**

◯ **Setting times will vary depending on the size of pan or mold used, as well as the flavoring added. Dust the uppermost surface with a little more of the coating mixture—this will stop it from drying out too much while setting. Let the marshmallow set in a cool dry place, but do not put it into the refrigerator.**

◯ **If you don't want to cut the set marshmallow immediately, lift it out of the pan, using the lining paper, and put it into a large, airtight container. Do not remove the lining paper until you are ready to cut and coat the marshmallow.**

Keeping qualities

ALTHOUGH BEST EATEN WITHIN A COUPLE OF DAYS OF MAKING, UNDECORATED MARSHMALLOWS (WITHOUT A COATING, SUCH AS CHOCOLATE OR CARAMEL) WILL EASILY KEEP FOR UP TO FIVE DAYS. STORE IN AN AIRTIGHT CONTAINER IN A COOL, DRY PLACE. MARSHMALLOWS ALSO FREEZE EXCEPTIONALLY WELL. FREEZE IN A SINGLE LAYER IN A FREEZER-PROOF CONTAINER FOR UP TO ONE MONTH. DEFROST AT ROOM TEMPERATURE FOR 30 MINUTES—1 HOUR, DEPENDING ON THE SIZE.

Essential ingredients

Sugar

Everyday granulated sugar is ideal for the basic sugar syrup. The even grains will slowly dissolve into the liquid when gently heated.

Egg whites

Always use fresh eggs at room temperature. Chilled egg whites will not incorporate as much air when beaten, so remember to remove the eggs from the refrigerator at least 30 minutes before you start cooking.

Gelatin

Unflavored powdered gelatin (as used in all of the recipes that follow) dissolved in hot water gives the marshmallow its soft set and springy texture. Always add the gelatin into the liquid, never the other way around, or it won't dissolve properly.

Confectioners' sugar and cornstarch

All marshmallows need to be lightly coated with a mixture of confectioners' sugar and cornstarch to prevent them from sticking to absolutely everything! Use equal quantities of each and sift together through a sifter or fine-mesh strainer to remove any lumps.

Veggie friendly

There are vegetarian alternatives to gelatin available, such as agar—follow package directions to prepare, then add to the sugar syrup in place of the gelatin solution.

Basic equipment

Food mixer

The secret to a light and voluminous marshmallow mixture is to beat, beat, beat! If you plan to make a lot of marshmallows, then a freestanding mixer with a beater attachment is essential. A handheld mixer will do the job just as well, as long as it has variable speed settings.

Candy thermometer

To make sure that the sugar syrup is boiled to the correct temperature, you'll need to invest in a candy thermometer. The syrup needs to reach the "firm ball" stage, 244-248°F, which will be clearly marked on the thermometer.

Heavy saucepan

Use a medium, heavy saucepan to make the sugar syrup. It needs to be deep enough for the candy thermometer to clip to the side of the pan without touching the bottom.

Heatproof bowls and liquid measuring cup

These are essential because a boiled sugar syrup is extremely hot and will melt plastic equipment. To pour the hot syrup into the beaten egg whites in a steady stream use a large heatproof liquid measuring cup with a firm handle.

Cake pans and silicone molds

The marshmallow mixture needs to be set in a shallow pan or mold. Always prepare by greasing thoroughly with a flavourless oil or nonstick cooking spray. Line with parchment paper, then regrease and dust with the cornstarch-and-confectioners' sugar mixture. Silicone cake pans or individual silicone cups have the added benefit of being very flexible, so the set marshmallows are really easy to remove.

Sharp knife

A long, thin, sharp knife will make it easy to cut the set marshmallow into pieces. The knife needs to be lightly greased to prevent it from sticking. Alternatively, a greased pizza cutter or a pair of sharp scissors will also do the job.

Cookie cutters

Marshmallow that has been set in a jellyroll pan is thin enough to be stamped out in shapes using cookie cutters. Choose simple shapes and use a pastry brush to thoroughly grease the cutter. Press the cutter down firmly with the palm of your hand, then gently lift out the shaped marshmallow.

Safety first

Of course, common sense rules in the kitchen (especially when you're working with hot sugar). Be careful when boiling the syrup and adding it to the egg whites because it will be extremely hot!

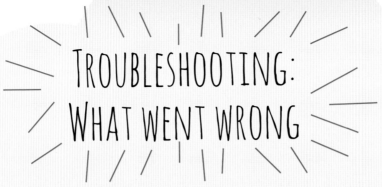

TROUBLESHOOTING: WHAT WENT WRONG

MARSHMALLOW MESS: Help! There are sugar crystals in the syrup.

SUPERSWEET SOLUTION: The sugar was not thoroughly dissolved in the liquid, or the syrup was stirred during boiling. To prevent sugar crystals from forming on the inside of the saucepan, brush lightly with cold water just above the bubbling syrup.

MARSHMALLOW MESS: Oh no! My marshmallow mixture isn't increasing in volume!

SUPERSWEET SOLUTION: All the air was knocked out of the egg whites when the hot syrup was added too quickly. Add the syrup in a very slow trickle at first, then in a thicker stream as the volume of the mixture increases.

MARSHMALLOW MESS: Why are my marshmallows so dense?

SUPERSWEET SOLUTION: The mixture was not beaten for long enough or was overbeaten after the flavorings were added.

MARSHMALLOW MESS: My mallows turned soggy in storage ...

SUPERSWEET SOLUTION: The mixture was not beaten for long enough. If this doesn't help, try reducing the volume of liquid used for softening the gelatin, but only by 1–2 tablespoons.

Featherlight,
fluffy, puffy treats

Basic Vanilla
MARSHMALLOWS

Makes: 25
Prep: 40 minutes
Cook: 20 minutes
Set: 4-5 hours

Ingredients

SUNFLOWER OIL, FOR GREASING

1 TABLESPOON CORNSTARCH

1 TABLESPOON CONFECTIONERS' SUGAR

1 CUP COLD WATER

2¼ CUPS GRANULATED SUGAR

½ CUP HOT WATER

¼ CUP UNFLAVORED POWDERED GELATIN

2 EXTRA-LARGE EGG WHITES

1 TEASPOON VANILLA EXTRACT

1. Lightly oil a shallow 8-inch square cake pan. Line the bottom and two sides with parchment paper, then lightly oil the paper.

2. To make the coating, sift the cornstarch and confectioners' sugar into a bowl. Use a little of this mixture to dust the lined pan, tapping it firmly to coat the bottom and sides completely.

3. To make the marshmallow, put the cold water and granulated sugar into a small, deep saucepan. Heat gently, stirring continuously with a wooden spoon, until the sugar has dissolved.

4. Bring the syrup to a boil and boil, without stirring, for about 5 minutes, until the mixture reaches around 248°F on a candy thermometer (the firm ball stage).

5. Meanwhile, put the hot water into a small bowl, sprinkle the gelatin over it, and stir until dissolved and the liquid is clear. Put the egg whites into the bowl of a free-standing electric mixer and beat until they hold stiff peaks.

6. When the syrup has reached the correct temperature, remove the pan from the heat and add the gelatin mixture—it will fizz and bubble. Let stand for a few seconds, then slowly pour the syrup into a large, heatproof measuring cup (be careful—the mixture will be extremely hot).

... CONTINUES ON PAGE 14

12

2.

4.

5.

6.

7.

13

7. Turn the mixer on to low speed and gradually add the hot syrup to the egg whites in a slow thin stream, beating continuously. When all the syrup has been added, increase the speed to high and beat for 10 minutes, until the mixture is thick and glossy and leaves a thick trail on the surface when the beaters are lifted.

8. Beat in the vanilla extract.

9. Pour the mixture into the prepared pan and use a rubber spatula to gently level the surface.

10. Lightly dust the top with a little of the coating mixture. Let set, uncovered, in a cool, dry place for 4-5 hours.

11. Run the tip of a lightly greased knife along the unlined sides of the pan to release the marshmallow. Using the lining paper, gently lift out the marshmallow and place on a cutting board.

12. Cut into 25 or 36 squares, frequently wiping and regreasing the knife. Lightly dust the squares with the remaining coating mixture. Store in an airtight container for up to five days.

9.

10.

Very Vanilla
MARSHMALLOW TOPPERS

Makes: 24
Prep: 40 minutes
Cook: 20 minutes
Set: 3-4 hours

Ingredients

SUNFLOWER OIL, FOR GREASING

1 TABLESPOON CORNSTARCH

1 TABLESPOON CONFECTIONERS' SUGAR

1 CUP COLD WATER

2¼ CUPS GRANULATED SUGAR

½ CUP HOT WATER

¼ CUP UNFLAVORED POWDERED GELATIN

2 EXTRA-LARGE EGG WHITES

1 TEASPOON VANILLA EXTRACT

UNSWEETENED COCOA POWDER,
FOR DUSTING

1. Lightly oil a 9 x 13-inch jellyroll pan. Line the bottom and two short sides with parchment paper, then lightly oil the paper.

2. To make the coating, sift the cornstarch and confectioners' sugar into a bowl. Use a little of this mixture to dust the lined pan, tapping it firmly to coat the bottom and sides completely.

3. Follow the basic recipe (see page 12) to make the marshmallow. Pour the mixture into the prepared pan and gently level the surface. Lightly dust the top with a little of the coating mixture. Let set, uncovered, in a cool, dry place for 3-4 hours.

4. Run the tip of a lightly greased knife along the unlined sides of the pan to release the marshmallow. Using the lining paper, gently lift out the marshmallow sheet and place on a cutting board.

5. Lightly grease a large snowflake cookie cutter and use to stamp out 14 shapes, washing, drying, and regreasing the cutter frequently. Use a small star-shape cutter to stamp out about ten stars from the remaining marshmallow. Toss all the shapes in the remaining coating mixture. Store in an airtight container for up to five days.

6. To serve, dust with cocoa powder and float the marshmallows on top of hot drinks, such as milky coffee or hot chocolate.

3.

5.

6.

Milk Chocolate
MARSHMALLOW STIRRERS

Makes: 25
Prep: 45 minutes
(plus cooling)
Cook: 25 minutes
Set: 4–5 hours

Ingredients

SUNFLOWER OIL, FOR GREASING

1 TABLESPOON CORNSTARCH

1 TABLESPOON CONFECTIONERS' SUGAR

1 CUP COLD WATER

2¼ CUPS GRANULATED SUGAR

½ CUP HOT WATER

¼ CUP UNFLAVORED POWDERED GELATIN

2 EXTRA-LARGE EGG WHITES

1 TEASPOON VANILLA EXTRACT

TO DECORATE

6 OUNCES MILK CHOCOLATE,
BROKEN INTO PIECES

SPRINKLES

YOU WILL ALSO NEED

25 LOLLIPOP STICKS

1. Lightly oil a 7-inch square cake pan (at least 2 inches deep). Line the bottom and two sides with parchment paper, then lightly oil the paper.

2. To make the coating, sift the cornstarch and confectioners' sugar into a bowl. Use a little of this mixture to dust the lined pan, tapping it firmly to coat the bottom and sides completely.

3. Follow the basic recipe (see page 12) to make the marshmallow. Pour the mixture into the prepared pan and gently level the surface. Lightly dust with a little of the coating mixture. Let set, uncovered, in a cool, dry place for 4–5 hours.

4. Run the tip of a lightly greased knife along the unlined sides of the pan to release the marshmallow. Using the lining paper, gently lift out the marshmallow and place on a cutting board. Cut into 25 squares with a lightly greased knife. Lightly dust the squares with the remaining coating mixture.

5. To decorate, put the chocolate into a double boiler or a heatproof bowl set over a saucepan of gently simmering water and heat until melted. Remove from the heat and stir until smooth. Let cool for 10 minutes. Line a baking sheet with parchment paper.

6. Gently push a lollipop stick into each marshmallow. Dip in the melted chocolate, turning to coat, then shake gently to let the excess run off.

7. Roll each dipped marshmallow in the sprinkles to coat. Place on the prepared baking sheet and let stand in a cool place to set. Store in an airtight container for up to five days.

18

4.

6.

7.

19

Pink & Puffy
MARSHMALLOW CRISPS

Makes: 24
Prep: 45 minutes
(plus cooling)
Cook: 20 minutes
Set: 3–4 hours

Ingredients

SUNFLOWER OIL, FOR GREASING

1 TABLESPOON CORNSTARCH

1 TABLESPOON CONFECTIONERS' SUGAR

1 CUP COLD WATER

2¼ CUPS GRANULATED SUGAR

½ CUP HOT WATER

¼ CUP UNFLAVORED POWDERED GELATIN

2 EXTRA-LARGE EGG WHITES

1 TEASPOON VANILLA EXTRACT

PINK FOOD COLORING PASTE

5 CUPS PUFFED RICE CEREAL

1. Lightly oil a 9 x 13-inch jellyroll pan. Line the bottom and two short sides with parchment paper, then lightly oil the paper. Line a large baking sheet with parchment paper.

2. To make the coating, sift the cornstarch and confectioners' sugar into a bowl. Use a little of this mixture to dust the lined pan, tapping it firmly to coat the bottom and sides completely.

3. Follow the basic recipe (see page 12) to make the marshmallow. Add a little of the food coloring paste to color the mixture pale pink, then fold in the cereal. Pour the mixture into the prepared pan and gently level the surface. Lightly dust the top with a little of the coating mixture. Let set, uncovered, in a cool, dry place for 3–4 hours.

4. Run the tip of a lightly greased knife along the unlined sides of the pan to release the marshmallow. Using the lining paper, gently lift out the marshmallow sheet and place on a cutting board.

5. Lightly grease a 2-inch round cutter and use to stamp out 24 circles, washing, drying, and regreasing the cutter frequently. Toss the circles in the remaining coating mixture. Store in an airtight container for up to two days.

YOU CAN MAKE MARSHMALLOW CRISPS WITH ANY OF THE FLAVORED MARSHMALLOW RECIPES THAT FOLLOW—JUST ADD PUFFED RICE CEREAL TO THE MIXTURE!

2.

3.

4.

21

Rainbow Stripe
MARSHMALLOWS

Makes: 36
Prep: 50 minutes
Cook: 20 minutes
Set: 4-5 hours

Ingredients

SUNFLOWER OIL, FOR GREASING

1 TABLESPOON CORNSTARCH

1 TABLESPOON CONFECTIONERS' SUGAR

1 CUP COLD WATER

2¼ CUPS GRANULATED SUGAR

½ CUP HOT WATER

¼ CUP UNFLAVORED POWDERED GELATIN

2 EXTRA-LARGE EGG WHITES

1 TEASPOON VANILLA EXTRACT

VIOLET, PINK, GREEN, AND ORANGE FOOD COLORING PASTE

1. Lightly oil a shallow 8-inch square cake pan. Line the bottom and two sides with parchment paper, then lightly oil the paper.

2. To make the coating, sift the cornstarch and confectioners' sugar into a bowl. Use a little of this mixture to dust the lined pan, tapping it firmly to coat the bottom and sides completely.

3. Follow the basic recipe (see page 12) to make the marshmallow. Divide the mixture evenly among four small bowls. Beat a little violet food coloring paste into one bowl. Spoon the colored marshmallow into the bottom of the prepared pan and gently level the surface with a small angled spatula.

4. Repeat the coloring and layering with the remaining bowls of mixture to create a rainbow effect. Work quickly before the marshmallow starts to set. Lightly dust the top layer of the marshmallow with a little of the coating mixture. Let set, uncovered, in a cool, dry place for 4-5 hours.

5. Run the tip of a lightly greased knife along the unlined sides of the pan to release the marshmallow. Using the lining paper, gently lift out the marshmallow and place on a cutting board.

6. Cut into 36 squares, wiping and regreasing the knife frequently. Lightly dust the squares with the remaining coating mixture. Store in an airtight container for up to five days.

3.

4.

6.

Sweetheart
MARSHMALLOW POPS

Makes: 25
Prep: 55 minutes (plus cooling)
Cook: 25 minutes
Set: 3–4 hours

Ingredients

SUNFLOWER OIL, FOR GREASING

1 TABLESPOON CORNSTARCH

1 TABLESPOON CONFECTIONERS' SUGAR

1 CUP COLD WATER

2¼ CUPS GRANULATED SUGAR

½ CUP HOT WATER

¼ CUP UNFLAVORED POWDERED GELATIN

2 EXTRA-LARGE EGG WHITES

2 TEASPOONS ROSE WATER

PINK FOOD COLORING PASTE

TO DECORATE

14 OUNCES PINK CANDY MELTS
OR 2 CUPS WHITE CHOCOLATE CHIPS

SPRINKLES

YOU WILL ALSO NEED

25 LOLLIPOP STICKS

1. Lightly oil a 9 x 13-inch jellyroll pan. Line the bottom and two short sides with parchment paper, then lightly oil the paper.

2. To make the coating, sift the cornstarch and confectioners' sugar into a bowl. Use a little of this mixture to dust the lined pan, tapping it firmly to coat the bottom and sides completely.

3. Follow the basic recipe (see page 12) to make the marshmallow, replacing the vanilla extract with rose water. Color the mixture pale pink with a little food coloring paste. Pour the mixture into the prepared pan and gently level the surface. Lightly dust the top with a little of the coating mixture. Let set, uncovered, in a cool, dry place for 3–4 hours.

4. Run the tip of a lightly greased knife along the unlined sides of the pan to release the marshmallow. Using the lining paper, gently lift out the marshmallow sheet and place on a cutting board.

5. Lightly grease a 1¾-inch heart-shape cutter and use to stamp out 25 hearts, washing, drying, and regreasing the cutter frequently. Toss the hearts in the remaining coating mixture.

... CONTINUES ON PAGE 26

3.

3.

6.

6. To decorate, place the candy melts in a double boiler or a large heatproof bowl set over a saucepan of gently simmering water and let stand until melted. Remove from the heat and stir until smooth. Let cool for 5 minutes. Line a large baking sheet with parchment paper.

7. Using two spoons, quickly dip a marshmallow heart, one at a time, in the melted mixture, turning to coat completely. Place on the prepared baking sheet and sprinkle with sprinkles. Let stand in a cool, dry place to set.

8. Carefully remove the hearts from the parchment paper and gently push a lollipop stick into the bottom of each heart. Store in an airtight container for up to five days.

IF A VALENTINE'S VIBE DOESN'T TICKLE YOU PINK, GIVE THESE DELICATE ROSE WATER POPS SOME PETAL POWER WITH A FLOWER-SHAPE COOKIE CUTTER.

OH SO CUTE!

Chai Tea & Vanilla
MINI MARSHMALLOWS

Ingredients

SUNFLOWER OIL, FOR GREASING

1 TABLESPOON CORNSTARCH

1 TABLESPOON CONFECTIONERS' SUGAR

1/2 TEASPOON GROUND GINGER

1/2 TEASPOON GROUND CLOVES

1/2 CUP COLD WATER

1/2 CUP COLD CHAI TEA,
MADE WITH 1 CHAI TEABAG

2 1/4 CUPS GRANULATED SUGAR

1/2 CUP HOT WATER

1/4 CUP UNFLAVORED POWDERED GELATIN

2 EXTRA-LARGE EGG WHITES

1 TEASPOON VANILLA EXTRACT

1 TEASPOON GROUND CARDAMOM
AND 1 TEASPOON GRATED NUTMEG,
FOR SPRINKLING

1. Lightly oil a 9 x 13-inch jellyroll pan. Line the bottom and two short sides with parchment paper, then lightly oil the paper.

2. To make the coating, sift the cornstarch, confectioners' sugar, ginger, and cloves into a bowl. Use a little of this mixture to dust the lined pan, tapping it firmly to coat the bottom and sides completely.

3. Follow the basic recipe (see page 12) to make the marshmallow, replacing half the cold water for the sugar syrup with the chai tea.

4. Pour the mixture into the prepared pan and gently level the surface. Sprinkle with the cardamom and nutmeg, then lightly dust the top with a little of the coating mixture. Let set, uncovered, in a cool, dry place for 3-4 hours.

5. Run the tip of a lightly greased knife along the unlined sides of the pan to release the marshmallow. Using the lining paper, gently lift out the marshmallow sheet and place on a cutting board.

6. Using a lightly greased mini star-shape cutter, stamp out about 50 shapes, washing, drying, and regreasing the cutter frequently. Toss the shapes in the remaining coating mixture. Store in an airtight container for up to five days.

2.

4.

6.

Peanut Butter Cup
MARSHMALLOWS

Makes: 42
Prep: 45 minutes
(plus cooling)
Cook: 25 minutes
Set: 2-3 hours

Ingredients

SUNFLOWER OIL, FOR GREASING

1 TABLESPOON CORNSTARCH

1 TABLESPOON CONFECTIONERS' SUGAR

1 CUP COLD WATER

2¼ CUPS GRANULATED SUGAR

½ CUP HOT WATER

¼ CUP UNFLAVORED POWDERED GELATIN

2 EXTRA-LARGE EGG WHITES

1 TEASPOON VANILLA EXTRACT

¾ CUP CHOPPED MIXED NUTS

TO DECORATE

8 OUNCES MILK CHOCOLATE, BROKEN INTO PIECES

⅓ CUP LIGHTLY TOASTED, BLANCHED PEANUTS

1. Lightly oil 42 silicone mini cupcake cups and put onto a large baking sheet. To make the coating, sift the cornstarch and confectioners' sugar into a bowl. Use a little of this mixture to dust each cup.

2. Follow the basic recipe (see page 12) to make the marshmallow. Fold in the nuts. Divide the mixture among the prepared cups. Lightly dust the tops with a little of the coating mixture. Let set, uncovered, in a cool, dry place for 2-3 hours.

3. Carefully remove the marshmallows from the cups. Lightly dust each one with the remaining coating mixture.

4. To decorate, put the chocolate in a double boiler or a heatproof bowl set over a saucepan of gently simmering water and heat until melted. Remove from the heat and stir until smooth. Let cool for 10 minutes.

5. Meanwhile, line a baking sheet with parchment paper. Holding each marshmallow by the bottom, briefly dip the top in the melted chocolate, then place on the prepared baking sheet. Top each marshmallow with a few toasted peanuts and let stand in a cool place to set. Store in an airtight container for up to five days.

Mocha
MARSHMALLOWS

Makes: 24
Prep: 45 minutes (plus cooling)
Cook: 25 minutes
Set: 3–4 hours

Ingredients

SUNFLOWER OIL, FOR GREASING

1 TABLESPOON CORNSTARCH

1 TABLESPOON CONFECTIONERS' SUGAR

1 CUP COLD WATER

2¼ CUPS GRANULATED SUGAR

½ CUP HOT BLACK COFFEE, MADE WITH 2 TEASPOONS INSTANT ESPRESSO COFFEE GRANULES

¼ CUP UNFLAVORED POWDERED GELATIN

2 EXTRA-LARGE EGG WHITES

1 TEASPOON VANILLA EXTRACT

TO DECORATE

4 OUNCES SEMISWEET CHOCOLATE, BROKEN INTO PIECES

2 TABLESPOONS FINELY GRATED SEMISWEET CHOCOLATE

1. Lightly oil a 9 x 13-inch jellyroll pan. Line the bottom and two short sides with parchment paper, then lightly oil the paper.

2. To make the coating, sift the cornstarch and confectioners' sugar into a bowl. Use a little of this mixture to dust the lined pan, tapping it firmly to coat the bottom and sides completely.

3. Follow the basic recipe (see page 12) to make the marshmallow, dissolving the gelatin in the hot coffee.

4. Pour the mixture into the prepared pan and gently level the surface. Lightly dust the top with a little more of the coating mixture. Let set, uncovered, in a cool, dry place for 3–4 hours.

5. Run the tip of a lightly greased knife along the unlined sides of the pan to release the marshmallow. Using the lining paper, gently lift out the marshmallow sheet and place on a cutting board. Cut into 24 squares, wiping and regreasing the knife frequently. Lightly dust the squares with the remaining coating mixture.

6. To decorate, put the chocolate pieces into a double boiler or a heatproof bowl set over a saucepan of gently simmering water. Heat until melted. Remove from the heat and stir until smooth. Let cool for 10 minutes. Line a baking sheet with parchment paper.

7. Dip each marshmallow square halfway into the melted chocolate, shaking gently to let the excess run off. Sprinkle with the grated chocolate. Place on the prepared baking sheet and let stand in a cool place to set. Store in an airtight container for up to five days.

3.

5.

7.

Chocolate & Hazelnut
MARSHMALLOWS

Makes: 25
Prep: 45 minutes
(plus cooling)
Cook: 25 minutes
Set: 4-5 hours

Ingredients

SUNFLOWER OIL, FOR GREASING

1 TABLESPOON CORNSTARCH

1 TABLESPOON CONFECTIONERS' SUGAR

1 CUP COLD WATER

2¼ CUPS GRANULATED SUGAR

½ CUP HOT WATER

¼ CUP UNFLAVORED POWDERED GELATIN

2 EXTRA-LARGE EGG WHITES

1 TEASPOON VANILLA EXTRACT

3 TABLESPOONS CHOCOLATE-AND-HAZELNUT SPREAD, WARMED

25 BLANCHED HAZELNUTS, TOASTED

TO DECORATE

4 OUNCES SEMISWEET CHOCOLATE, BROKEN INTO PIECES

1. Lightly oil a shallow 8-inch square cake pan. Line the bottom and two sides with parchment paper, then lightly oil the paper.

2. To make the coating, sift the cornstarch and confectioners' sugar into a bowl. Use this mixture to dust the lined pan, tapping it firmly to coat the bottom and sides completely.

3. Follow the basic recipe (see page 12) to make the marshmallow. Gently fold in the warmed chocolate-and-hazelnut spread.

4. Pour the mixture into the prepared pan and gently level the surface. Lightly dust the top with some of the coating mixture, then arrange the hazelnuts evenly on top of the marshmallow. Let set, uncovered, in a cool, dry place for 4-5 hours.

5. Run the tip of a lightly greased knife along the unlined sides of the pan to release the marshmallow. Using the lining paper, gently lift out the marshmallow and place on a cutting board. Cut into 25 squares, wiping and regreasing the knife frequently. Dust with the coating mixture.

6. To decorate, put the chocolate into a double boiler or a heatproof bowl set over a saucepan of gently simmering water and heat until melted. Remove from the heat and stir until smooth. Let cool for 10 minutes.

7. Spoon the chocolate into a paper pastry bag and snip off the end. Pipe lines of chocolate over the marshmallows. Let stand in a cool place to set. Store in an airtight container for up to five days.

3.

4.

7.

Cinnamon & Cocoa
MARSHMALLOWS

Ingredients

SUNFLOWER OIL, FOR GREASING

1 TABLESPOON CORNSTARCH

1 TABLESPOON CONFECTIONERS' SUGAR

1/2 TEASPOON COCOA POWDER

1/4 TEASPOON GROUND CINNAMON

1 CUP COLD WATER

2 1/4 CUPS GRANULATED SUGAR

1/2 CUP HOT WATER

1/4 CUP UNFLAVORED POWDERED GELATIN

2 EXTRA-LARGE EGG WHITES

1 1/2 TEASPOONS GROUND CINNAMON

3 TABLESPOONS UNSWEETENED COCOA POWDER BLENDED TO A PASTE WITH 3 TABLESPOONS HOT WATER

1. Lightly oil a shallow 8-inch square cake pan. Line the bottom and two sides with parchment paper, then lightly oil the paper.

2. To make the coating, sift the cornstarch, confectioners' sugar, cocoa powder, and cinnamon into a bowl. Use a little of this mixture to dust the lined pan, tapping it firmly to coat the bottom and sides completely.

3. Follow the basic recipe (see page 12) to make the marshmallow, omitting the vanilla extract.

4. Transfer half the marshmallow mixture to a separate bowl and gently fold in the ground cinnamon. Gradually fold the cocoa paste into the remaining mixture.

5. Drop alternate spoonfuls of the two mixtures into the prepared pan and gently level the surface. Swirl the two mixtures together with the tip of a knife. Let set, uncovered, in a cool, dry place for 4–5 hours.

6. Run the tip of a lightly greased knife along the unlined sides of the pan to release the marshmallow. Using the lining paper, gently lift out the marshmallow and place on a cutting board. Cut into 36 squares, wiping and regreasing the knife frequently. Lightly dust the bars with the coating mixture. Store in an airtight container for up to five days.

2.

4.

5.

White Choc & Peppermint
MARSHMALLOWS

Makes: 24
Prep: 45 minutes
(plus cooling)
Cook: 25 minutes
Set: 3-4 hours

Ingredients

SUNFLOWER OIL, FOR GREASING

1 TABLESPOON CORNSTARCH

1 TABLESPOON CONFECTIONERS' SUGAR

1 CUP COLD WATER

2¼ CUPS GRANULATED SUGAR

½ CUP HOT WATER

¼ CUP UNFLAVORED POWDERED GELATIN

2 EXTRA-LARGE EGG WHITES

FEW DROPS PEPPERMINT EXTRACT

4 OUNCES WHITE CHOCOLATE, BROKEN INTO PIECES

4 SMALL CANDY CANES, COARSELY CRUSHED

1. Lightly oil two 12-cup silicone cupcake pans and place on two baking sheets. To make the coating, sift the cornstarch and confectioners' sugar into a bowl. Use a little of this mixture to lightly dust each hole.

2. Follow the basic recipe (see page 12) to make the marshmallow, replacing the vanilla extract with the peppermint extract.

3. Put the chocolate into a double boiler or a heatproof bowl set over a saucepan of barely simmering water and heat until melted. Remove from the heat and stir until smooth. Let cool for 10 minutes, stirring occasionally.

4. Gently fold three-quarters of the melted chocolate into the marshmallow mixture. Spoon the mixture into the prepared pans.

5. Spoon a small swirl of the remaining melted chocolate onto each marshmallow and sprinkle with the crushed candy canes. Lightly dust the tops with a little of the coating mixture. Let set, uncovered, in a cool, dry place for 3-4 hours.

6. Carefully remove the marshmallows from the pans. Lightly dust the bottom and sides with the remaining coating mixture. Store in an airtight container for up to five days.

3.

4.

5.

Caramel Bite
MARSHMALLOWS

Makes: 25
Prep: 45 minutes
Cook: 20 minutes
Set: 4-5 hours

Ingredients

SUNFLOWER OIL, FOR GREASING

1 TABLESPOON CORNSTARCH

1 TABLESPOON CONFECTIONERS' SUGAR

1 CUP COLD WATER

2¼ CUPS GRANULATED SUGAR

½ CUP HOT WATER

¼ CUP UNFLAVORED POWDERED GELATIN

2 EXTRA-LARGE EGG WHITES

1 TEASPOON VANILLA EXTRACT

8 TABLESPOONS DULCE DU LECHE
(CARAMEL SAUCE)

¼ CUP MILK CHOCOLATE CHIPS

1. Lightly oil a shallow 8-inch square cake pan. Line the bottom and two sides with parchment paper, then lightly oil the paper.

2. To make the coating, sift the cornstarch and confectioners' sugar into a bowl. Use this mixture to dust the lined pan, tapping it firmly to coat the bottom and sides completely.

3. Follow the basic recipe (see page 12) to make the marshmallow. Gently fold in 3 tablespoons of the dulce du leche.

4. Pour one-third of the marshmallow mixture into the prepared pan, then dot with tiny blobs of dulce du leche. Make two more layers with the remaining marshmallow and dulce du leche, then drag a toothpick through the marshmallow to create a swirled effect.

5. Sprinkle the chocolate chips over the marshmallow mixture, then lightly dust the top with a little of the coating mixture. Let set, uncovered, in a cool, dry place for 4-5 hours.

6. Run the tip of a lightly greased knife along the unlined sides of the pan to release the marshmallow. Using the lining paper, gently lift out the marshmallow and place on a cutting board.

7. Cut into 25 squares, wiping and regreasing the knife frequently. Lightly dust the squares with the remaining coating mixture. Store in an airtight container for up to five days.

4.

5.

7.

Cookie Sandwich
MARSHMALLOWS

Makes: 20
Prep: 1 hour 15 mins
(plus chilling & cooling
Cook: 40 minutes
Set: 3-4 hours

Ingredients

SUNFLOWER OIL, FOR GREASING

1 TABLESPOON CORNSTARCH

1 TABLESPOON CONFECTIONERS' SUGAR

1 CUP COLD WATER

2¼ CUPS GRANULATED SUGAR

½ CUP HOT WATER

¼ CUP UNFLAVORED POWDERED GELATIN

2 EXTRA-LARGE EGG WHITES

1 TEASPOON VANILLA EXTRACT

COOKIES

1 STICK BUTTER, SOFTENED, PLUS EXTRA FOR GREASING

¼ CUP GRANULATED SUGAR

1 EGG YOLK

1⅓ CUPS ALL-PURPOSE FLOUR, PLUS EXTRA FOR DUSTING

9 OUNCES SEMISWEET CHOCOLATE, BROKEN INTO PIECES

1. Lightly oil a 9 x 13-inch jellyroll pan. Line the bottom and two short sides with parchment paper then lightly oil the paper.

2. To make the coating, sift the cornstarch and confectioners' sugar into a bowl. Use a little of this mixture to dust the lined pan, tapping it firmly to coat the bottom and sides completely.

3. Follow the basic recipe (see page 12) to make the marshmallow. Pour the mixture into the prepared pan and gently level the surface. Lightly dust the top with a little of the coating mixture. Let set, uncovered, in a cool, dry place for 3–4 hours.

4. Meanwhile, make the cookies. Put the butter and sugar into a bowl and beat with an electric mixer until pale and creamy. Beat in the egg yolk, then sift in the flour and mix to a soft dough. Knead lightly until smooth, then wrap in plastic wrap and chill in the refrigerator for 45 minutes.

5. Preheat the oven to 350°F. Grease two large baking sheets. Roll out the dough on a lightly floured work surface to about ¼ inch thick and use a 2½-inch cloud-shape cutter to stamp out 40 cookies, rerolling the dough as necessary. Place on the prepared baking sheets and chill in the refrigerator for 30 minutes.

... CONTINUES ON PAGE 44

6.

7.

9.

43

6. Bake in the preheated oven for 10–12 minutes or until pale golden brown. Let cool on the sheets for 1–2 minutes, then transfer to a wire rack to cool completely.

7. Put the chocolate into a double boiler or a heatproof bowl set over a saucepan of gently simmering water and heat until melted. Remove from the heat and stir until smooth. Let cool for 10 minutes. Dip one side of each cookie in the melted chocolate, then place on a wire rack set over a baking sheet. Chill in the refrigerator until set.

8. To assemble the sandwich cookies, run the tip of a lightly greased knife along the unlined sides of the pan to release the marshmallow. Using the lining paper, gently lift out the marshmallow sheet and slide onto a cutting board.

9. Lightly grease the cloud cutter and use to stamp out 20 cloud shapes, washing, drying, and regreasing the cutter frequently. Toss all the cloud shapes in the remaining coating mixture. Sandwich each marshmallow between two of the chocolate-coated cookies. Store in an airtight container for up to five days.

OUR CRISP, CHOCOLATY COOKIES ARE SHAPED LIKE CLOUDS, BUT YOU CAN USE ANY SIMPLE COOKIE CUTTER FOR BOTH THE COOKIE BASE AND THE MARSHMALLOW MIDDLE.

FLUFFY FILLING

Pina Colada
MARSHMALLOWS

Makes: 35
Prep: 45 minutes
Cook: 20 minutes
Set: 4-5 hours

Ingredients

SUNFLOWER OIL, FOR GREASING

1 TEASPOON CORNSTARCH

1 TEASPOON CONFECTIONERS' SUGAR

1½ CUPS UNSWEETENED DRY COCONUT

PINK FOOD COLORING PASTE

½ CUP PINEAPPLE JUICE

½ CUP COLD WATER

2¼ CUPS GRANULATED SUGAR

½ CUP HOT WATER

¼ CUP UNFLAVORED POWDERED GELATIN

2 EXTRA-LARGE EGG WHITES

2 TABLESPOONS COCONUT LIQUEUR OR RUM, WARMED

YELLOW FOOD COLORING PASTE

1. Lightly oil a shallow 7 x 11-inch baking pan. Line the bottom and two short sides with parchment paper, then lightly oil the paper.

2. To make the coating, sift the cornstarch and confectioners' sugar into a bowl. Use a little of this mixture to dust the lined pan, tapping it firmly to coat the bottom and sides completely.

3. Put the coconut into a resealable plastic food bag with a tiny amount of pink food coloring paste. Seal the bag and rub it thoroughly between the palms of your hands until the coconut is evenly colored pale pink. Sprinkle half the coconut into the bottom of the prepared pan, reserving the remainder.

4. Follow the basic recipe (see page 12) to make the marshmallow, replacing half the cold water for the sugar syrup with the pineapple juice and omitting the vanilla extract. Beat in the liqueur and then beat in a little food coloring paste to turn the mixture pale yellow.

5. Pour the mixture into the prepared pan. Level the surface and sprinkle over the remaining pink coconut to cover the top completely, pressing down gently. Let set, uncovered, in a cool, dry place for 4-5 hours.

6. Run the tip of a lightly greased knife along the unlined sides of the pan to release the marshmallow. Using the lining paper, gently lift out the marshmallow and place on a cutting board. Cut into 35 squares, wiping and regreasing the knife frequently. Store in an airtight container for up to five days.

3.

4.

6.

Mojito
MARSHMALLOWS

Makes: 25
Prep: 45 minutes
(plus cooling)
Cook: 30 minutes
Set: 4-5 hours

Ingredients

SUNFLOWER OIL, FOR GREASING

1 TABLESPOON CORNSTARCH

1 TABLESPOON CONFECTIONERS' SUGAR

1 CUP COLD WATER

5 FRESH MINT SPRIGS

JUICE OF 1 LARGE LIME

2¼ CUPS GRANULATED SUGAR

¼ CUP UNFLAVORED POWDERED GELATIN

2 EXTRA-LARGE EGG WHITES

1 TABLESPOON WHITE RUM, WARMED

GREEN FOOD COLORING PASTE

1 TEASPOON FINELY GRATED LIME ZEST

1 TEASPOON FINELY CHOPPED
FRESH MINT

1. Lightly oil a shallow 8-inch square cake pan. Line the bottom and two sides with parchment paper, then lightly oil the paper.

2. To make the coating, sift the cornstarch and confectioners' sugar into a bowl. Use this mixture to dust the lined pan, tapping it firmly to coat the bottom and sides completely.

3. Put the water and mint into a saucepan over low heat and heat until almost boiling. Remove from the heat and let cool completely. Strain into a measuring cup, topping up with cold water to make 1 cup, then set aside. Pour the lime juice into a clean, heatproof measuring cup and add enough boiling water to make ½ cup liquid. Pour into a small saucepan and heat over low heat.

4. Follow the basic recipe (see page 12) to make the marshmallow, using the mint-flavored water for the syrup. Dissolve the gelatin in the hot lime juice mixture and omit the vanilla extract. Beat in the rum and a little food coloring paste to color the marshmallow pale green. Fold in the lime zest and chopped mint.

5. Pour the mixture into the prepared pan and gently level the surface. Lightly dust the top with a little of the coating mixture. Let set, uncovered, in a cool, dry place for 4-5 hours.

6. Run the tip of a lightly greased knife along the unlined sides of the pan to release the marshmallow. Using the lining paper, gently lift out the marshmallow and place on a cutting board. Cut into 25 squares, wiping and regreasing the knife frequently. Lightly dust the squares with the coating mixture. Store in an airtight container for up to five days.

3.

4.

5.

Bourbon & Brown Sugar
MARSHMALLOWS

Makes: 24
Prep: 40 minutes
Cook: 20 minutes
Set: 3–4 hours

Ingredients

SUNFLOWER OIL, FOR GREASING

1 TABLESPOON CORNSTARCH

1 TABLESPOON CONFECTIONERS' SUGAR

1 CUP COLD WATER

2¼ CUPS GRANULATED SUGAR

½ CUP HOT WATER

¼ CUP UNFLAVORED POWDERED GELATIN

2 EXTRA-LARGE EGG WHITES

1 TEASPOON VANILLA EXTRACT

2 TABLESPOONS BOURBON, WARMED

¼ CUP RAW BROWN SUGAR

1. Lightly oil a 9 x 13-inch jellyroll pan. Line the bottom and two short sides with parchment paper, then lightly oil the paper.

2. To make the coating, sift the cornstarch and confectioners' sugar into a bowl. Use a little of this mixture to dust the lined pan, tapping it firmly to coat the bottom and sides completely.

3. Follow the basic recipe (see page 12) to make the marshmallow. Gradually beat in the bourbon.

4. Pour the mixture into the prepared pan and gently level the surface. Lightly dust the top with a little of the coating mixture. Let set, uncovered, in a cool, dry place for 3–4 hours.

5. Run the tip of a lightly greased knife along the sides of the pan to release the marshmallow. Using the lining paper, gently lift out the marshmallow sheet and place on a cutting board.

6. Lightly grease a 2-inch round cutter and stamp out 24 circles, washing, drying, and regreasing the cutter frequently. Lightly dust the top and bottom of the marshmallows with the remaining coating mixture.

7. Put the raw brown sugar onto a flat plate. Roll the edge of each marshmallow around in the sugar to coat. Store in an airtight container for up to five days.

6.

7.

3.

Amaretto Crunch
MARSHMALLOWS

Ingredients

SUNFLOWER OIL, FOR GREASING

1 TEASPOON CORNSTARCH

1 TEASPOON CONFECTIONERS' SUGAR

1½ CUPS CRUSHED AMARETTI COOKIES

1 CUP COLD WATER

2¼ CUPS GRANULATED SUGAR

½ CUP HOT WATER

¼ CUP UNFLAVORED POWDERED GELATIN

2 EXTRA-LARGE EGG WHITES

1 TABLESPOON AMARETTO LIQUEUR, WARMED

1. Lightly oil a shallow 8-inch square cake pan. Line the bottom and two sides with parchment paper, then lightly oil the paper.

2. To make the coating, sift the cornstarch and confectioners' sugar into a bowl. Use this mixture to dust the lined pan, tapping it firmly to coat the bottom and sides completely. Spread one-third of the crushed cookies in an even layer in the bottom of the pan.

3. Follow the basic recipe (see page 12) to make the marshmallow, omitting the vanilla extract. Gradually beat in the liqueur.

4. Pour the mixture into the prepared pan and gently level the surface. Sprinkle another one-third of the crushed cookies over the top to cover the surface. Let set, uncovered, in a cool, dry place for 4-5 hours.

5. Run the tip of a lightly greased knife along the unlined sides of the pan to release the marshmallow. Using the lining paper, gently lift out the marshmallow and place on a cutting board.

6. Cut the marshmallow into 25 squares, wiping and regreasing the knife frequently. Coat the squares in the remaining crushed cookies. Store in an airtight container for up to five days.

2.

4.

6.

Irish Cream
MARSHMALLOWS

Makes: 20
Prep: 45 minutes
(plus cooling)
Cook: 25 minutes
Set: 3–4 hours

Ingredients

SUNFLOWER OIL, FOR GREASING

1 TABLESPOON CORNSTARCH

1 TABLESPOON CONFECTIONERS' SUGAR

1 CUP COLD WATER

2¼ CUPS GRANULATED SUGAR

½ CUP HOT WATER

¼ CUP UNFLAVORED POWDERED GELATIN

2 EXTRA-LARGE EGG WHITES

2 TABLESPOONS IRISH CREAM LIQUEUR, WARMED

TO DECORATE

8 OUNCES SEMISWEET CHOCOLATE, BROKEN INTO PIECES

UNSWEETENED COCOA POWDER, FOR DUSTING

1. Lightly oil a 9 x 13-inch jellyroll pan. Line the bottom and two short sides with parchment paper, then lightly oil the paper.

2. To make the coating, sift the cornstarch and confectioners' sugar into a bowl. Use a little of this mixture to dust the lined pan, tapping it firmly to coat the bottom and sides completely.

3. Follow the basic recipe (see page 12) to make the marshmallow, omitting the vanilla extract. Gradually beat in the liqueur.

4. Pour the mixture into the prepared pan and gently level the surface. Lightly dust the top with a little of the coating mixture. Let set, uncovered, in a cool, dry place for 3–4 hours.

5. Run the tip of a lightly greased knife along the unlined sides of the pan to release the marshmallow. Using the lining paper gently lift out the marshmallow sheet and place on a cutting board.

6. Lightly grease a 2¹/₂-inch heart-shape cutter. Use to stamp out 20 heart shapes, washing, drying, and regreasing the cutter frequently. Toss the hearts in the coating mixture.

7. To decorate, put the chocolate into a double boiler or a heatproof bowl set over a saucepan of gently simmering water and heat until melted. Remove from the heat and stir until smooth. Let cool for 10 minutes. Line a baking sheet with parchment paper

8. Dip one side of each marshmallow in the melted chocolate to coat. Place on the prepared baking sheet and let stand in a cool place to set. Dust lightly with a little cocoa powder. Store in an airtight container for up to five days.

4.

6.

8.

Egg Nog
MARSHMALLOWS

Makes: 24
Prep: 40 minutes
Cook: 20 minutes
Set: 3-4 hours

Ingredients

SUNFLOWER OIL, FOR GREASING

1 TABLESPOON CORNSTARCH

1 TABLESPOON CONFECTIONERS' SUGAR

1 CUP COLD WATER

2¼ CUPS GRANULATED SUGAR

½ CUP HOT WATER

¼ CUP UNFLAVORED POWDERED GELATIN

2 EXTRA-LARGE EGG WHITES

1 TEASPOON VANILLA EXTRACT

1½ TABLESPOONS BRANDY, WARMED

1 TEASPOON GROUND CINNAMON

1 TEASPOON GRATED NUTMEG

1. Lightly oil 24 star-shape silicone cupcake cups and place on a large baking sheet. To make the coating, sift the cornstarch and confectioners' sugar into a bowl. Use a little of this mixture to dust each cup.

2. Follow the basic recipe (see page 12) to make the marshmallow. Gradually beat in the brandy and half the cinnamon and nutmeg. Spoon the mixture into the prepared cups.

3. Mix together the remaining cinnamon and nutmeg and sprinkle a little on top of each marshmallow. Using a toothpick, gently swirl the spices through the marshmallow. Lightly dust the tops with a little of the coating mixture. Let set, uncovered, in a cool, dry place for 3-4 hours.

4. Carefully remove the marshmallows from the cups. Lightly dust the bottom and sides of each one with the remaining coating mixture. Store in an airtight container for up to five days.

FLOAT A COUPLE OF THESE MINI MARSHMALLOWS ON TOP OF A MUG OF HOT CHOCOLATE, WITH PLENTY OF WHIPPED CREAM— IT'S SO DELISH!

Rum & Raisin
MARSHMALLOWS

Makes: 35
Prep: 40 minutes
(plus soaking)
Cook: 20 minutes
Set: 4-5 hours

Ingredients

1/2 CUP RAISINS

2 TABLESPOONS DARK RUM, WARMED

SUNFLOWER OIL, FOR GREASING

1 TABLESPOON CORNSTARCH

1 TABLESPOON CONFECTIONERS' SUGAR

1 CUP COLD WATER

2 1/4 CUPS GRANULATED SUGAR

1/2 CUP HOT WATER

1/4 CUP UNFLAVORED POWDERED GELATIN

2 EXTRA-LARGE EGG WHITES

2 TEASPOONS COFFEE AND CHICORY EXTRACT

1. Place the raisins and rum in a small bowl and let soak for 2 hours.

2. Lightly oil a shallow 7 x 11-inch baking pan. Line the bottom and two short sides with parchment paper, then lightly oil the paper.

3. To make the coating, sift the cornstarch and confectioners' sugar into a bowl. Use a little of this mixture to dust the lined pan, tapping it firmly to coat the bottom and sides completely.

4. Follow the basic recipe (see page 12) to make the marshmallow, replacing the vanilla extract with the coffee and chicory extract.

5. Drain the raisins and fold half of them into the marshmallow, then pour the mixture into the prepared pan. Level the surface and sprinkle with the remaining raisins. Lightly dust the top with some of the coating mixture. Let set, uncovered, in a cool, dry place for 4-5 hours.

6. Run the tip of a lightly greased knife along the unlined sides of the pan to release the marshmallow. Using the lining paper, gently lift out the marshmallow and place on a cutting board. Cut into 35 squares, wiping and regreasing the knife frequently. Lightly dust the squares with the remaining coating mixture. Store in an airtight container for up to five days.

1.

4.

5.

Toffee Apple
MARSHMALLOW POPS

Makes: 36
Prep: 50 minutes
(plus cooling)
Cook: 25 minutes
Set: 4-5 hours

Ingredients

SUNFLOWER OIL, FOR GREASING

1 TABLESPOON CORNSTARCH

1 TABLESPOON CONFECTIONERS' SUGAR

1/2 CUP COLD WATER

1/2 CUP APPLE JUICE

2 1/4 CUPS GRANULATED SUGAR

1/2 CUP HOT WATER

1/4 CUP UNFLAVORED POWDERED GELATIN

2 EXTRA-LARGE EGG WHITES

1 1/2 TEASPOONS GROUND CINNAMON

TOFFEE

2/3 CUP GRANULATED SUGAR

3 TABLESPOONS COLD WATER

YOU WILL ALSO NEED

36 LOLLIPOP STICKS

1. Lightly oil a shallow 8-inch cake pan. Line the bottom and sides with parchment paper then lightly oil the paper.

2. To make the coating, sift the cornstarch and confectioners' sugar into a bowl. Use a little of this mixture to dust the lined pan, tapping it firmly to coat the bottom and sides completely.

3. Follow the basic recipe (see page 12) to make the marshmallow, replacing half the cold water for the sugar syrup with apple juice and omitting the vanilla extract.

4. Pour the mixture into the prepared pan and gently level the surface. Sprinkle with the cinnamon, then lightly dust the top with a little of the coating mixture. Let set, uncovered, in a cool, dry place for 4-5 hours. Line a baking sheet with parchment paper

5. Using the lining paper, gently lift out the marshmallow and place on a cutting board. Cut into 36 squares with a lightly greased knife, wiping and regreasing the knife frequently. Dust the squares lightly with the remaining coating mixture. Place the marshmallows on the prepared baking sheet.

... CONTINUES ON PAGE 62

ADD SOME CRUNCH BY SPRINKLING CRUSHED COOKIES ON TOP OF THE TOFFEE— GINGERSNAPS ADD A DELICIOUS CRISP BITE.

60

5.

6.

7.

6. To make the toffee, put the sugar and water into a small, heavy saucepan and heat gently, stirring, until the sugar has dissolved. Increase the heat and boil rapidly for 3-4 minutes, without stirring, until the syrup turns to a golden caramel. Swirl the pan to make sure of even cooking. Remove from the heat and let stand for 1-2 minutes.

7. Using a spoon, quickly drizzle the hot toffee over the marshmallows (be careful, because the toffee will be extremely hot). Let stand in a cool place until the toffee has set. Lift each marshmallow from the baking sheet and gently push a lollipop stick into each one. Serve within a few hours of decorating.

WITHOUT THE TOFFEE DRIZZLE, THE MARSHMALLOWS CAN BE STORED IN AN AIRTIGHT CONTAINER FOR UP TO FIVE DAYS. DECORATE WITH THE TOFFEE ON THE DAY OF SERVING.

Pumpkin & Pecan
MARSHMALLOWS

Makes: 25
Prep: 50 minutes (plus cooling)
Cook: 30 minutes
Set: 4-5 hours

Ingredients

SUNFLOWER OIL, FOR GREASING

2 TEASPOONS CORNSTARCH

2 TEASPOONS CONFECTIONERS' SUGAR

1 CUP COLD WATER

2¼ CUPS GRANULATED SUGAR

½ CUP HOT WATER

¼ CUP UNFLAVORED POWDERED GELATIN

2 EXTRA-LARGE EGG WHITES

1 TEASPOON VANILLA EXTRACT

½ CUP CANNED PUMPKIN PUREE, WARMED

2 TEASPOONS GROUND ALLSPICE

ORANGE FOOD COLORING PASTE

SUGAR-COATED PECANS

1 TABLESPOON EGG WHITE, BEATEN

1 TEASPOON VANILLA EXTRACT

¼ CUP FIRMLY PACKED LIGHT BROWN SUGAR

¾ CUP PECANS

1. Lightly oil a shallow 8-inch square cake pan. Line the bottom and two sides with parchment paper, then lightly oil the paper.

2. To make the coating, sift the cornstarch and confectioners' sugar into a bowl. Use this mixture to dust the lined pan, tapping it firmly to coat the bottom and sides completely.

3. Follow the basic recipe (see page 12) to make the marshmallow. Gently fold in the warmed pumpkin puree and allspice. Fold in a little food coloring paste to color the mixture orange.

4. Pour the mixture into the prepared pan and gently level the surface. Lightly dust the top with some of the coating mixture. Let set, uncovered, in a cool, dry place for 4-5 hours.

5. Meanwhile, make the sugar-coated pecans. Preheat the oven to 300°F. Line a baking sheet with parchment paper. Mix together the egg white, vanilla extract, and sugar in a small bowl, then add the nuts and stir to coat. Spread the coated nuts evenly on the prepared sheet. Bake in the preheated oven for 25-30 minutes, turning once, until crisp and golden brown. Let cool completely.

6. Run the tip of a lightly greased knife along the unlined sides of the pan to release the marshmallow. Using the lining paper, gently lift out the marshmallow and place on a cutting board. Cut into 25 squares, wiping and regreasing the knife frequently.

7. Finely chop the sugar-coated nuts and spread on a flat plate. Dip every side of each marshmallow in the chopped nuts to coat. Serve on the day of decorating.

3.

5.

7.

Undecorated, the marshmallows will keep in an airtight container for up to five days. The sugar-coated pecans will keep in an air-tight container for up to one week.

Peanut Butter & Jelly
MARSHMALLOWS

Makes: 25
Prep: 40 minutes
Cook: 20 minutes
Set: 4–5 hours

Ingredients

SUNFLOWER OIL, FOR GREASING

1 TABLESPOON CORNSTARCH

1 TABLESPOON CONFECTIONERS' SUGAR

1 CUP COLD WATER

2¼ CUPS GRANULATED SUGAR

½ CUP HOT WATER

¼ CUP UNFLAVORED POWDERED GELATIN

2 EXTRA-LARGE EGG WHITES

1 TEASPOON VANILLA EXTRACT

¼ CUP CHUNKY PEANUT BUTTER, SOFTENED

3 TABLESPOONS RASPBERRY JELLY OR SEEDLESS RASPBERRY PRESERVES

3 TABLESPOONS BLANCHED PEANUTS, TOASTED AND CHOPPED

1. Lightly oil a shallow 8-inch square cake pan. Line the bottom and two sides with parchment paper, then lightly oil the paper.

2. To make the coating, sift the cornstarch and confectioners' sugar into a bowl. Use a little of this mixture to dust the lined pan, tapping it firmly to coat the bottom and sides completely.

3. Follow the basic recipe (see page 12) to make the marshmallow. Gently fold in the peanut butter.

4. Pour half the mixture into the prepared pan, then top with 1 tablespoon of the jelly and swirl through the mixture with the tip of a knife. Repeat with the remaining marshmallow mixture and the remaining jelly.

5. Swirl the jelly through the marshmallow with the tip of a knife. Sprinkle with the chopped peanuts. Lightly dust the top with a little of the coating mixture. Let set, uncovered, in a cool, dry place for 4–5 hours.

6. Run the tip of a lightly greased knife along the unlined sides of the pan to release the marshmallow. Using the lining paper, gently lift out the marshmallow and place on a cutting board. Cut into 25 squares, wiping and regreasing the knife frequently. Lightly dust the squares with the remaining coating mixture. Store in an airtight container for up to five days.

Gingerbread
MARSHMALLOWS

Ingredients

SUNFLOWER OIL, FOR GREASING

1 TABLESPOON CORNSTARCH

1 TABLESPOON CONFECTIONERS' SUGAR

2 TEASPOONS GROUND GINGER

1 CUP COLD WATER

1¼ CUPS GRANULATED SUGAR

1 CUP FIRMLY PACKED LIGHT BROWN SUGAR

½ CUP HOT WATER

¼ CUP UNFLAVORED POWDERED GELATIN

2 EXTRA-LARGE EGG WHITES

1. Lightly oil a 9 x 13-inch jellyroll pan. Line the bottom and two short sides with parchment paper, then lightly oil the paper.

2. To make the coating, sift the cornstarch, confectioners' sugar, and 1 teaspoon of ground ginger into a bowl. Use a little of this mixture to dust the lined pan, tapping it firmly to coat the bottom and sides completely.

3. Follow the basic recipe (see page 12) to make the marshmallow, replacing half the granulated sugar with brown sugar and omitting the vanilla extract. Fold in the remaining ground ginger.

4. Pour the mixture into the prepared pan and gently level the surface. Lightly dust the top with a little of the coating mixture. Let set, uncovered, in a cool, dry place for 3-4 hours.

5. Run the tip of a lightly greased knife along the unlined sides of the pan to release the marshmallow. Using the lining paper, gently lift out the marshmallow sheet and place on a cutting board.

6. Lightly grease a small gingerbread man cookie cutter. Use to stamp out 24 shapes, washing, drying, and regreasing the cutter frequently. Toss the gingerbread men in the coating mixture. Store in an airtight container for up to five days.

3.

6.

2.

Cookies & Cream
MARSHMALLOWS

Makes: 35
Prep: 40 minutes
Cook: 20 minutes
Set: 4–5 hours

Ingredients

SUNFLOWER OIL, FOR GREASING

1 TEASPOON CORNSTARCH

1 TEASPOON CONFECTIONERS' SUGAR

18 SMALL DOUBLE CHOCOLATE CHIP COOKIES

1 CUP COLD WATER

2¼ CUPS GRANULATED SUGAR

½ CUP HOT WATER

¼ CUP UNFLAVORED POWDERED GELATIN

2 EXTRA-LARGE EGG WHITES

1 TEASPOON VANILLA EXTRACT

1. Lightly oil a shallow 7 x 11-inch baking pan. Line the bottom and two short sides with parchment paper, then lightly oil the paper.

2. To make the coating, sift the cornstarch and confectioners' sugar into a bowl. Use a little of this mixture to dust the lined pan, tapping it firmly to coat the bottom and sides completely.

3. Arrange 15 of the cookies in the bottom of the prepared pan. Finely crush the remaining cookies and set aside.

4. Follow the basic recipe (see page 12) to make the marshmallow. Pour the mixture into the pan. Level the surface and sprinkle with the crushed cookies to cover the top completely. Let set, uncovered, in a cool, dry place for 4–5 hours.

5. Run the tip of a lightly greased knife along the unlined sides of the pan to release the marshmallow. Using the lining paper, gently lift out the marshmallow and place on a cutting board. Cut into 35 squares, wiping and regreasing the knife frequently. Store in an airtight container for up to five days.

3.

4.

5.

S'mores
MARSHMALLOW POPS

Ingredients

SUNFLOWER OIL, FOR GREASING

1 TABLESPOON CORNSTARCH

1 TABLESPOON CONFECTIONERS' SUGAR

1 CUP COLD WATER

2¼ CUPS GRANULATED SUGAR

½ CUP HOT WATER

¼ CUP UNFLAVORED POWDERED GELATIN

2 EXTRA-LARGE EGG WHITES

1 TEASPOON VANILLA EXTRACT

TO DECORATE

6 OUNCES MILK CHOCOLATE,
BROKEN INTO PIECES

2 GRAHAM CRACKERS, FINELY CRUSHED

YOU WILL ALSO NEED

25 LOLLIPOP STICKS

1. Lightly oil a 7-inch square cake pan (at least 2 inches deep). Line the bottom and sides with parchment paper, then lightly oil the paper.

2. To make the coating, sift the cornstarch and confectioners' sugar into a bowl. Use a little of this mixture to dust the lined pan, tapping it firmly to coat the bottom and sides completely.

3. Follow the basic recipe (see page 12) to make the marshmallow. Pour the mixture into the prepared pan and gently level the surface. Lightly dust the top with a little of the coating mixture. Let set, uncovered, in a cool, dry place for 4-5 hours. Preheat the broiler to medium-high.

4. Run the tip of a lightly greased knife along the unlined sides of the pan to release the marshmallow. Using the lining paper, gently lift out the marshmallow and place on a cutting board. Cut into 25 squares with a lightly greased knife, wiping and regreasing the knife frequently. Lightly dust the squares with the remaining coating mixture.

5. Lightly toast the marshmallows under preheated broiler, turning frequently until just golden brown (do this briefly or they will melt and lose their shape). Alternatively, use a chef's blowtorch. Let cool.

... CONTINUES ON PAGE 74

72

5.

6.

7.

73

6. To decorate, put the chocolate into a double boiler or a heatproof bowl set over a saucepan of gently simmering water and heat until melted. Remove from the heat and stir until smooth. Let cool for 10 minutes.

7. Meanwhile, line a board with parchment paper. Dip one end of each marshmallow in the melted chocolate, turning to coat, then shaking gently to let the excess run off. Sprinkle the chocolate with crushed crackers, then place on the prepared board. Let stand in a cool place to set. Gently push a lollipop stick into the chocolate end of each marshmallow. Store in an airtight container for up to five days.

A CLASSIC CAMPFIRE COMBO—
CHOCOLATE, MARSHMALLOW, AND
GRAHAM CRACKERS ARE HARD TO BEAT!

Zesty Lemon
MARSHMALLOWS

Ingredients

SUNFLOWER OIL, FOR GREASING

1 TABLESPOON CORNSTARCH

1 TABLESPOON CONFECTIONERS' SUGAR

1 CUP COLD WATER

2¼ CUPS GRANULATED SUGAR

¼ CUP UNFLAVORED POWDERED GELATIN

½ CUP HOT LEMON JUICE

2 EXTRA-LARGE EGG WHITES

FINELY GRATED ZEST OF 1 LEMON

YELLOW FOOD COLORING PASTE

2 TABLESPOONS WHITE SPRINKLES

1. Lightly oil a shallow 8-inch square cake pan. Line the bottom and two sides with parchment paper, then lightly oil the paper.

2. To make the coating, sift the cornstarch and confectioners' sugar into a bowl. Use this mixture to dust the lined pan, tapping it firmly to coat the bottom and sides completely.

3. Follow the basic recipe (see page 12) to make the marshmallow, dissolving the gelatin in the hot lemon juice instead of hot water and omitting the vanilla extract.

4. Transfer one-third of the mixture to a separate bowl and set aside. Fold the lemon zest into the remaining mixture and beat in a little food coloring paste to color it pale yellow.

5. Pour the yellow mixture into the prepared pan and level the surface, then spoon the white mixture over the top and gently level with a small rubber spatula. Sprinkle with the sprinkles, then lightly dust the top with a little of the coating mixture. Let set, uncovered, in a cool, dry place for 4–5 hours.

6. Run the tip of a lightly greased knife along the unlined sides of the pan to release the marshmallow. Using the lining paper, gently lift out the marshmallow and place on a cutting board. Cut into 36 squares, wiping and regreasing the knife frequently. Lightly dust the squares with the remaining coating mixture. Store in an airtight container for up to five days.

3.

5.

6.

YUM!

HOMEMADE
pillows OF
SUGAR

This edition published by Parragon Books Ltd in 2013 and distributed by

Parragon Inc.
440 Park Avenue South, 13th Floor
New York, NY 10016
www.parragon.com/lovefood

LOVE FOOD is an imprint of Parragon Books Ltd

ISBN 978-1-4723-2918-9

Printed in China

Project managed by Alice Blackledge
Designed by Beth Kalynka
Recipes, introduction, and food styling by Angela Drake
Photography by Clive Streeter
Edited by Fiona Biggs

Notes for the Reader
This book uses standard kitchen measuring spoons and cups. All spoon and cup measurements are level unless otherwise indicated. Unless otherwise stated, milk is assumed to be whole and eggs are large.

The times given are only an approximate guide. Preparation times differ according to the techniques used by different people and the cooking times may also vary from those given.

Recipes using raw or very lightly cooked eggs should be avoided by infants, the elderly, pregnant women, convalescents, and anyone with a weakened immune system. Pregnant and breast-feeding women are advised to avoid eating peanuts and peanut products. People with nut allergies should be aware that some of the prepared ingredients used in the recipes in this book may contain nuts. Always check the packaging before use.